It's Not Alright - For Children

A Basic Guide To Acceptable Behavior

Written By David Long

Illustrated by David Villaluz

ISBN: 978-1478160908

Table of Contents

It's Not Alright - For Children   **1**

A Basic Guide To Acceptable Behavior   *1*

Dedication   *5*

To the parent   *6*

It's not alright run by the swimming pool.   *8*

It's not alright to jump and play on the stairs.   *11*

It's not alright to hit someone.   *12*

It's not alright to tell a lie.   *15*

It's not alright to touch the stove.   *16*

It's not alright to touch someone in their 'private places.'   *19*

It's not alright to look into the sun.   *20*

It's not alright to put things in your ears.   *23*

It's not alright to touch sharp knives.   *24*

It's not alright to say naughty words.   *27*

It's not alright to eat the dog's food.   *28*

It's not alright to pull hair.   *31*

It's not alright to take something that isn't yours.   *32*

It's not alright to kick or hurt the dog.   *35*

It's not alright to throw food.   *36*

It's not alright to make fun of other people.   *39*

It's not alright to bite people.   *40*

It's not alright to break glass.   *43*

It's not alright to stink.   *44*

It's not alright to be a bully.   *47*

It's not alright to forget to flush the toilet.   *48*

It's not alright to chew with an open mouth.   *51*

It's not alright to forget to brush your teeth.   *53*

It's not alright to throw a tantrum.   *54*

It's not alright to beg for stuff in the store.   *57*

It's not alright to paint your sister.   *58*

It's not alright to color on the walls.   *61*

It's not alright to play with matches or a lighter.   *62*

It's not alright to touch fire.   *65*

It's not alright to leave the house without telling someone.   *67*

It's not alright to forget to put away the milk.   68

It's not alright to forget to feed the pet.   71

It's not alright to forget to turn off the water.   72

It's not alright to wear your underwear on the outside.   75

It's not alright to stick your fingers into the outlets on the wall.   76

It's not alright to whack your brother.   79

It's not alright to be the captain.   80

It's not alright to climb on the furniture.   83

It's not alright to eat dirt.   84

It's not alright to put things into your mouth that don't belong there.   87

It's not alright to play in the street.   88

It's not alright to be mean to little animals.   91

It's not alright to carry the cat by its neck.   92

It's not alright to cross the street outside the crosswalk.   95

It's not alright to get bad grades.   96

It's not alright to hide from mommy in the store.   99

It's not alright to play and make loud noises in Church.   101

It's not alright to run in the house.   102

It's not alright to run with scissors.   105

It's not alright to spit.   106

It's not alright to talk to strangers.   109

It's not alright to throw rocks.   110

It's not alright to throw things at people.   113

It's not alright to waste food.   114

The End   116

Dedication

It's Not Alright - for Children is dedicated to my mom and dad who raised me to suffer the natural consequences of my actions – good and bad.

To the parent

When I was growing up and learning how to behave, it was completely acceptable for corporal punishment when I did something 'bad.' A good spanking, restriction to the house, banishment to my bedroom or being *grounded* from sports and social activities. I also suffered 'natural consequences' for my actions.

Nowadays, there's a fine line between physical punishment and abuse. We have to use more creative discipline. Timeouts, no cell phone or computer use, and still some amount of restriction. Or a just good 'talking-to.'

So what's a parent to do? How do you correct your child's negative behavior or just teach them about rules to live by in today's world?

It's Not Alright – for Children will help with some of those discipline issues. It gives you a tool to sit and talk to your child about what's appropriate and what's not appropriate. It is a *basic training* manual for life, if you will. Not every anecdote will fit your child's behavior or *your* sense of what's right and wrong. But there are 54 little behavioral snippets that most children will experience at some time.

So come on in and have fun. Use the book as one creative source of raising your child and opening conversation. If it works for you and you have teens, the second in a series is called *It's Not Alright – For Teens – an Intermediate Guide To Acceptable Behavior.* And if you have a significant other,

It's Not Alright For Adults – An Advanced Guide To Acceptable Behavior.

It's not alright run by the swimming pool.

Kids jump in and out of the pool and splash water on the sides. Everyone gets in and out of the pool and drips *more* water around the edges. This makes the edges around the pool very slippery. You could fall if you run. You could hurt yourself if you fall. Bang your head. Skin your knees and elbows. Bump your tailbone. And that could put an end to all the fun you're having. The sidewalks around the edges of the swimming pool were made for walking. That's why it's not ok to run at the pool.

It's not alright to jump and play on the stairs.

If you were supposed to jump down the stairs, they would have made them differently. They would put a ramp on the top for a good takeoff so that you could spread your arms and really soar. They would put fluffy pillows at the bottom for a feather-soft landing, because crashes are no fun at all. There aren't any stop signs or roads up there either, so how would you know where to go? Nope, stairs are not so great for jumping down or playing because they just weren't made for that. Stairs were made for taking one step at a time. Up. And down.

It's not alright to hit someone.

It is never okay to hit someone. People were not made for being hit. It hurts. If people were made to be hit, then they would have protective equipment built right in. People would come equipped with helmets and shoulder pads like a football player, or maybe with chest protector and pads like a catcher in baseball. Children can hit lots of things, like a home run in baseball or a hole-in-one in golf. People can hit the books, hit the road, or have a hit record, but it is not okay to hit another person. It is never okay to hit.

It's not alright to tell a lie.

The truth is the truth. It is the story of what happened. It doesn't need to be invented, because it invents itself. That's not a child's job. A child's job is to tell about what happened the way it happened. If children make up their own story that is different than what happened then it is called a lie. No one likes some one who lies because no one ever knows if what they say is a lie or the truth. Imagination is making up our own truth but we never pretend that make believe is real. It is not okay to invent the truth.

Telling a lie is different than lying down for a nap. Even though it is the same word it has different meanings. Telling a lie is when someone makes up the truth. Knowing the difference between the truth and a lie can be tricky sometimes. Telling a lie is making something up and saying it is what really happened. Okay? Let's tell the truth. Most lies we tell to keep us from getting in trouble. Sometimes people pretend that they didn't do something because they are afraid they will get in trouble, that's a lie. And it is not okay for children to tell a lie.

It's not alright to touch the stove.

Some things are good to be afraid of. The stove is one of them. Stoves are meant for cooking. They get really super-duper hot and that's how they help to cook food like hot dogs and scrambled eggs. Hands and fingers are not hotdogs and were not meant to be cooked. If your fingers were meant to be cooked there would be finger buns like hot dog buns. They don't make finger buns because fingers were not meant to be cooked like hot dogs. That's why it is not okay to touch the stove.

It's not alright to touch someone in their 'private places.'

The rule is that wherever there is underwear is not okay. It is nice to hold hands or hug one another. People shake hands to say hello or agree to something. There are lots and lots of nice ways to touch someone. Touching someone in one of THOSE places is NOT a nice way to touch. People get really mad and there's big, BIG trouble on this one. It is a big deal. That is why It's not okay to touch someone in one of THOSE places.

It's not alright to look into the sun.

The sun is so powerful that it makes the very daytime warm up. The sun gives the plants energy to grow big and strong. The sun is so bright that it makes the daytime happen. Our poor little eyeballs are just not strong enough to look into the sun. Our eyeballs work great for seeing the stars in the sky, but they are not strong enough to look into the sun and not get hurt. When we go outside to play in the sun, we have to wear sunblock to protect our skin, but they don't make sunblock for our eyeballs. I don't want to get my eyeballs sunburned by looking at the sun. That doesn't sound fun at all. It is not okay to look right into the sun.

It's not alright to put things in your ears.

Your ears were meant for hearing sounds like chirping birds, roaring thunder, and brilliant music. Ears were not meant for eating things like carrots or broccoli. If ears were meant for eating they would come with teeth to chew up the food. Ears don't come with teeth. They weren't meant for eating, they were meant for hearing. Sounds are the only things that ears were meant to eat. It is not okay for children to put anything in your ears except sounds.

It's not alright to touch sharp knives.

Knives are really sharp tools that were meant to cut things. Knives are used to cut our meat, to slice cheese, and to chop vegetables. Fingers were meant to stay in one piece, of course. All around our bodies is a thin covering like a balloon that protects us. It is called skin. Like a balloon that holds the air inside, our skin keeps our insides, inside us. Knives are really good tools for popping balloons and they are really good for cutting our skin and letting the insides out. That's why it is not okay for children to touch sharp things like knives.

It's not alright to say naughty words.

You know what words I'm talking about. We all know that there are some words that we shouldn't use. It gets real confusing. Sometimes we hear those words. It seems to bother some people more than others. Sometimes we get in trouble and sometimes we don't. Some people use those words all the time and they don't get in trouble. How in the world is a young child supposed to know? Children are not supposed to know about that stuff. That is why it is not okay for children to use THOSE words.

It's not alright to eat the dog's food.

No matter what you do, people are not dogs and dogs are not people. Children don't have tails that wag, tongues that flop around, and they don't have hair on their face. Dogs can't cook or say words or even use the bathroom. Dogs sure are fun to play with and they sure are happy creatures. It is real important to take care of a dog by feeding and watering it every day. Like children, dogs sure like to be loved. No matter how much we love dogs, they will never be people and people will never be dogs. Dog food is made for dogs, not people. If it were it would say "people food" on the package. It is not okay for children to eat dog food.

It's not alright to pull hair.

I know that sometimes it seems almost irresistible, as if a giant force of nature is attracting you like a magnet to those dangly pigtails. I know, I've been there too. Inside my head I can imagine pulling on that long hair or swinging around on it like a trapeze at the circus. It is a fun thought to have, but if I let it out of my head and actually do it, there's nothing good that can happen. Hair was not meant to be pulled. There is not one good reason for pulling hair. No one likes to have their hair pulled because it hurts. Pulling hair always hurts and always makes sisters or mommy and daddy get mad. That is why it is not okay for children to pull hair.

It's not alright to take something that isn't yours.

Some things are yours, like your toothbrush or underwear. Some things are not yours, like my toothbrush and my underwear. Sometimes its hard to tell what is yours and what is not. Some things belong to both of us. Some things are yours and I can use them like they are mine as long as I'm careful. That's called sharing. It can all be very confusing. If you take something that isn't yours without asking first, that is called stealing. There is nothing good about stealing. It is never a good thing. Everybody gets mad and there's big, BIG trouble for the person that does it. It is not okay for children to take something that isn't theirs.

It's not alright to kick or hurt the dog.

Soccer balls are meant to be kicked, kickballs are meant to be kicked, footballs are meant to be kicked, but dogs and little animals are not meant to be kicked. Or hurt. Dogs were meant to be loved and hugged and cuddled and petted. Dogs were meant to play games like chase and fetch and to run, and jump, and play. Dogs are not people and they don't speak English like we do. Sometimes it is hard to get a dog to do what you want, because they just don't understand. Sometimes dogs get so excited that they get too silly. Dogs were meant for lots of things like being a persons best friend, but they were not made for kicking. It is not okay for children to hit the dog.

It's not alright to throw food.

Food wasn't meant for throwing except in special cases by trained professionals. Watching your mashed potatoes and gravy splat on grandma's forehead and drip down her face is one of those thoughts that is fun to have inside your head, but not so great if you actually try it. Watching your Jell-O drip down your sisters nose is another one of those thoughts that is better left inside your head. There are many things that work better inside the imagination, throwing food is one of them. It is not okay for children to throw food.

It's not alright to make fun of other people.

Other people have feelings just like you do. The words you say to someone else can help them to feel good things, like happiness or joy, or not so good things, like sadness or anger. When you make fun of people it does not make them happy or help them to like you more. It can really hurt their feelings and make them not want to be your friend. You don't like it when people make fun of you. So you shouldn't make fun of them. No one wants to be friends with someone that makes fun of them. That's why it is not okay for children to make fun of other people.

It's not alright to bite people.

Biting is not okay ever, never, NEVER! It is okay to bite into an apple or a juicy strawberry. It is okay to bite your peanut butter and jelly sandwich. It is never okay to bite people. Or pets. The teeth in your mouth are made for chewing your food up into little pieces when you eat. Wild animals like lions, tigers, and bears bite, but people don't bite. When you bite someone it hurts them and there is nothing good that can come from that. There's not even one good reason to bite someone. That's why it's not ok to bite.

It's not alright to break glass.

Glass is pretty neat stuff. It's there but you can see right through it. Glass lets the sunlight shine right through it and still keeps the cold air outside. They make all kinds of things out of glass, like cups to drink from, light bulbs that turn on when you flip the switch, and windows in the car that go up and down. Eye glasses help people see better with their eyes. Glass is very useful to people, but there is one truth about glass that must be told. Glass breaks. It is easy to break glass. When glass breaks it comes apart into smaller pieces that have very, VERY sharp edges. Broken glass is dangerous because it is so sharp. It can cut you just by touching it. Broken glass is a little scary, even for grown-ups. That is why it is not okay for children to break glass.

It's not alright to stink.

Some things smell good to people, like radiant springtime
flowers and fancy perfume. Some things smell bad to people,
like a skunk or a dirty diaper. Okay, okay, poop is smelly too.
The bathroom can be a bad smelling place, that's why they
make that smelly good spray and why we have to wash our
hands before leaving. We don't want to take any of that smell
with us outside the bathroom. Workers at the fish-guts
factory have to really scrub hard when they get home,
because no one wants to be around someone that smells like
fish guts. It is hard to be friends with someone that smells
like a fish gut factory. That's why it is not okay to stink.

It's not alright to be a bully.

Being a bully is when one child makes themselves **FEEL BIG** by making someone else feel small. Being a bully can be big, **BIG** trouble. Being a bully is a little bit like having a mean boss. They tell you to do things that make you feel bad about yourself. No one wants to feel bad about themselves. You want to feel good about yourself. No one likes someone that makes you feel small. There's just nothing good that can come from that. No one likes a bully. If you act like a bully, then all you are doing is giving other people a reason to **NOT** like you. That is why it is not okay to be a bully.

It's not alright to forget to flush the toilet.

You can forget a lot of things and it doesn't bother anyone else, but forgetting to flush the toilet is one that bothers everyone else. If you forget to flush the toilet, the next person that enters will discover what you left in there. No one wants that. If you forget to flush, you are doing something that no one likes. That shiny handle on the toilet was put there to be used not forgotten. You can forget what 6 + 7 equals, you can forget how to spell "crocodile," and you can forget to raise your hand before talking, but every single person on the planet earth wants you to remember to flush. It is not okay to forget to flush the toilet.

It's not alright to chew with an open mouth.

It is a safety thing. If you leave the widow open the warm air can go out, and if you leave the door of the refrigerator open then all the cold air goes out. If you forget to put the top of a container back on then all the important stuff can fall out all over the place. And unless you remember to close your mouth when you chew your food, all that food can fall out. Food was made to be eaten, not spilled out of your mouth. Food is like the gas in a car, it gives you energy to run and jump and play. Food was meant to go into your body not onto your body. That is why it is not okay to chew with an open mouth.

It's not alright to forget to brush your teeth.

Teeth are important tools and they need to be taken care of by brushing them. We use our teeth to chew up our food into smaller pieces so that we can swallow it. Chewing is important part of getting the energy we need to get through the day, but it sure can be a messy business. Chewing gets out teeth all dirty. We need to clean our teeth by brushing them. Sometimes the air coming out of your mouth when you breath smells like dirty teeth and yesterdays lunch. No one likes someone who's breath smells like yesterdays lunch. A clean mouth is important. That's why it is not okay to forget to brush your teeth.

It's not alright to throw a tantrum.

Throwing a temper tantrum is when a young child looses control of themselves. Sometimes there is crying and shrieking and yelling and stuff. People don't like to see tantrums. It makes them feel uncomfortable. The thing about tantrums is that they never work. This is the one and only thing children need to know about tantrums, they never work. You never get what you want. Tantrums only get you in more trouble. Pretty soon in the growing up process all kids have to learn this lesson, it is not okay to throw a temper tantrum.

It's not alright to beg for stuff in the store.

Asking is not begging. It is okay to ask. Asking doesn't mean getting what you ask for. Asking for something and getting it are two different things. If you ask many times, over and over again, that's called begging. Begging is not okay. It's tricky to know how much asking makes into begging, but you should be able to tell by the look on the face of the person driving the cart. Grown-ups sure know when too much asking becomes begging, because it embarrasses and bothers them. Embarrassing and bothering grown-ups in a store is sure something that begging can do very quickly. That is why it is not okay to beg for stuff in the store.

It's not alright to paint your sister.

Blue is just not the right color at all. It is only okay to paint your sister pink and sometimes a little dash of purple stripes. No, that's not right! It is not okay to paint your sister at all in any color! Lots of things were meant to be painted, like signs and paintings, houses and cars, and walls, but not sisters. Sisters were not meant for painting. This is one of those thoughts that is so fun inside your head but if you try to do it there's just nothing good that can come from it. No matter how fun it is to imagine, it is not okay to paint your sister.

It's not alright to color on the walls.

Walls are not meant to be colored on. Walls like to stand there and hold up pictures. Walls are made to keep things like the kitchen and the bathroom apart. Walls are a great place to put closets and doors and windows. Walls are not made for putting crayons or markers on them. Crayons are great to use on coloring books, sketch pads and coloring paper. Markers, chalks, paints, and pencils work really well making creations on paper, but they just weren't made for walls. People weren't made to be a swimming pool and walls weren't made for being colored on. Making creations on walls is not okay to do.

It's not alright to play with matches or a lighter.

Matches and lighters are tools that people use to make fire.
It is much easier to use a match or a lighter than it is to rub
two sticks together like the cavemen did. Matches and
lighters are important tools used on heaters and stoves. Fire
can really mess things up. Fire can burn down buildings and
destroy everything inside. Fire can burn people and burns
really hurt. Fire can be used in really good ways, but fire was
not meant to be used by children and that it why it is not
okay to play with matches or a lighter.

It's not alright to touch fire.

Fire can be really pretty to look at. It lights up the area and glows all warm and comfortable looking. Fire is also really super-duper hot. It is so hot that if you touch fire it will burn your skin. Even though it is pretty to look at it is dangerous to touch. If you touch fire with something like a piece of paper, then the fire moves to the piece of paper. And if you drop the paper, the fire moves to the carpet on the floor and then to the walls and before you know it, everything is gone. Fire is an easy thing to make a little mistake that makes a big, BIG problem. That's why it is not okay to touch fire.

It's not alright to leave the house without telling someone.

Children always have some grown-up around that is responsible for them. That means that it is their job to keep you safe. If you leave the house without telling the grown-up that is responsible for you where you are going, how can they do their job? Sometimes it is okay to go outside and sometimes it is not okay. How in the world is a child supposed to know when it is okay and when it is not? Well, you are not supposed to know. That's the grown-up's job. It's the child's job to let someone know where they are all the time. It is not okay to leave the house without telling someone.

It's not alright to forget to put away the milk.

A big glass of milk with a plate of cookies is one of life's great pleasures. It is important to keep milk very cold in a refrigerator. If you forget to put milk away, and it gets warm, and it stays out for a while, then something very strange happens. It turns into something called rotten. Rotten is something that happens to food that is left out of the refrigerator and forgotten. Milk is the worst thing to allow to get rotten, because it smells worse than anything you ever had in your nose and if you drink it, it will make you turn green and throw up. That is why it is not okay for children to forget to put away the milk.

It's not alright to forget to feed the pet.

Lots of different animals make great pets, like dogs and cats, hamsters, guinea pigs, ferrets, goldfish, tweety-birds, horses, cows, and even elephants. The one common thing about all pets is that they need someone to take care of them. Pets need someone to feed and water them, and someone has to be the one that doesn't forget. Someone has to be responsible. If it is your job to feed the pet, that means that you are the one that has to be responsible and not forget. Your pet will not forget that he is hungry so you shouldn't either. If you forget, your pet will be hungry and that is not a good way to feel, is it? It is not okay for children to forget to feed him.

It's not alright to forget to turn off the water.

We use water for many things like drinking hot chocolate, taking a bubble bath, or washing our hands. Every time we use water we have to turn it on. We go to the faucet and turn on the cold water or the hot water. We go to the garden valve, turn the knob, and water comes out of the hose. All that water that comes out has to come from somewhere. It comes from the rain and flows into streams, rivers, and lakes all around you. We don't want to take too much away from the earth. Leaving the water on takes a lot of water away and doesn't help anyone. And water costs money. When we leave the water running, it wastes money. That is why it is not okay to forget to turn off the water.

It's not alright to wear your underwear on the outside.

There is just nothing about UNDERwear that is for wearing on the outside. Even if you didn't wear outerwear outside, because you only wore underwear out there, you would still be out there in only your underwear. Underwear means to be worn underneath your clothes. Underwear is not even worn on the outside by trained professionals. They don't even teach outside underwear wearing to trained professionals of any kind. I suppose you could wear outwear under there, but underwear must always remain under outerwear. That is why it is not okay for underwear to be worn over outerwear like pants.

It's not alright to stick your fingers into the outlets on the wall.

Those little electrical outlets are neat. We plug in all sorts of gadgets, gizmos, and important tools like that into those holes and they work. Then we pull the cord out and they don't work anymore. Grown-ups say it is because they are not plugged in. Inside those little holes is electricity. Electricity is like a bolt of lightning flashing down from a thunder cloud to the earth. Electricity is what makes all those gadgets work. Electricity is made for electric tools, not a little child's fingers. Sticking your fingers into outlets on the wall can hurt you. It can hurt you very badly. It is a big, BIG deal! Please do not hurt yourself by putting your fingers in the outlets on the wall.

It's not alright to whack your brother.

Okay, I know that sometimes you may think he deserves it, but it is never okay to whack your brother. I know that sometimes it seems like brothers are created to be whacked and that the one and only reason that they exist on the planet is to irritate you, but that still doesn't make it okay to whack your brother. It is the whacking that is not okay. It's not okay to whack much of anything. Maybe they should make some special whacking thing so that children could have something to whack besides brothers. That would make it much easier to not whack your brother. As it is today, the law is clear. It is not okay to whack your brother no matter how much he deserves it.

It's not alright to be the captain.

Children are beginners at most things. That's not to say that children aren't good at things, it's just saying that they don't have so much experience as older grown-up folks. To be the captain takes a lot of experience, going through lots of different things and seeing which ones work and which ones don't. The captain's job is to know what to do. It's always good if he's done it before and knows that it works. Children cannot be the captain because they are beginners and need to learn more. That's why it's not okay for children to be the captain.

It's not alright to climb on the furniture.

Spiderman can fly from building to building, Superman can leap over buildings in a single bound, but children break when they fall. That is the best reason not to let them dangle from high places or climb on the furniture. It may seem that movie and cartoon characters never hurt themselves when they fly around like superheroes, but in real life, children break. Children are not superheroes. It is important not to break young people. There is nothing good that can come from it. That is why it is not okay for children to dangle from high places or climb on furniture.

It's not alright to eat dirt.

The only thing that dirt is, is dirty. Dirty means to be like dirt. It's not a great idea to put dirty things into your mouth, so it's probably not a good idea to put dirt itself into your mouth. Dirt has stuff mixed in with it that can make you sick. Dirt is mostly crushed up rocks and it's hard to find nourishment in rocks. There's not any water in rocks either, so dirt will not quench a thirst. Dirt will make your mouth dirty. That is the only thing it does well. People weren't made to eat dirt or it would be better for us. That is why it is not okay for children to eat dirt.

It's not alright to put things into your mouth that don't belong there.

Our mouths are very important for many reasons. We breathe through our mouths. If we stop breathing we die. We don't want to stop breathing because we don't want to die. We want to make sure we always have enough clean fresh air to breath. If we put things in our mouth, they could get stuck when we swallow them down, and block the way for air to go in and out. That stops our breathing and we could die. This is a big, BIG safety thing. Putting things into your mouth that don't belong there could make you die. That is why it is not okay for children to put things in their mouth that don't belong there.

It's not alright to play in the street.

Playing in the road is not a good idea. Sometimes the front yard does not seem big enough and the street does. But streets are for cars and yards are for playing in. A park is a good place to play, but a road can be dangerous. When you are playing, you forget to pay attention to the traffic. Cars and trucks and motorcycles all zoom by sometimes really fast and if you are playing in the street you could get hit. It hurts to get hit and you could die! That is why it is not a good idea to play in the street.

It's not alright to be mean to little animals.

Little animals like cats and dogs and birds are our pets and friends. They like us and they trust us. They want us to be kind to them and not hurt them. Children who can hurt a small animal is a very sad and mean person inside. When they are mean to little creatures pretty soon the little animals will stay away because they are afraid. Sometimes a mean child who can hurt a little animal might also hurt something else. Like a brother or sister. Or a friend. Or more. Please don't hurt little animals.

It's not alright to carry the cat by its neck.

Kitties are so soft and warm and furry and cuddly. The kitty was meant to be loved and hugged and cuddled and petted. It likes being your friend. It was meant to roll around, play with string and chase dust and mice. It's no wonder you want to carry it everywhere you go. But kitties don't have handles like your suitcase. So how can you carry it safely? Not by it's neck, NO! You must carry Kitty safely like a baby curled up in your arms. Otherwise you could choke and hurt it and it could die. That is why it is not okay to carry Kitty by the neck.

It's not alright to cross the street outside the crosswalk.

See those painted stripes that go across the road at corners? It looks kind of like a zebra, doesn't it? The men painted the road for you to be safe. Like a path to walk from one corner to the next one. Grown-ups know that when you are in the crosswalk, they must slow or stop their cars to keep you safe. It is never a good idea to cross the street where there are no stripes for you to walk on. So don't ever get run over by a car, it hurts. That is why it's not alright to cross the street unless you are in a crosswalk.

It's not alright to get bad grades.

School is important. School helps you learn things that you need to know your whole life. Mommy and Daddy went to school and look how smart they are! You could be President if you went to school. But part of going to school is getting good grades in your classes. It is like having a shiny Sheriff's badge to wear. It makes you proud and shows everyone that you actually *do* know what you learned. If you get bad grades, it makes Mommy and Daddy sad and makes your life harder. Presidents and doctors and lawyers got good marks, so that's why it's not alright to get bad grades.

It's not alright to hide from mommy in the store.

Shopping with Mommy is fun. Up and down the aisles and so much to look at! But it is not a time to play hide-and-seek. Mommy is very busy buying food and things you need. Sometimes she has other thoughts in her head an it's not a time for playing games. Mommies and daddies get *very* scared when they can't find you. Thinking about losing their child makes them *very* nervous. Staying with Mommy and riding or holding on to the basket is very smart. That's why it's not okay to hide from Mommy in the store.

It's not alright to play and make loud noises in Church.

Church is a *very* quiet place to be. It is kind of like when you want to go to sleep and you want everything to be calm and quiet. That is how Church is. Calm and quiet. Except when everyone is singing. Then it is loud and joyful. People like to pray and think quiet thoughts in Church. You know how you like to just play quietly by yourself, sometimes? So playing or making loud noises in Church disturbs the quiet thoughts and prayers of the grown-ups, and they don't like that. And when you do that, people can't hear what the man in front is saying. That's why it's not okay to be loud in Church.

It's not alright to run in the house.

Running is a lot of fun! It is good exercise and gets us places fast! Sometimes we run just because it feels good. Dogs run, cats run, horses and cows and even birds run. Running in the house is not good. There are slippery floors in the house. And furniture. There are walls with sharp corners and tight curves. And there are people in the house. If you run indoors, you could fall and hurt yourself or run into someone and knock them over. Or you could break something and then you would be in big, BIG trouble. That's why running inside the house is not okay.

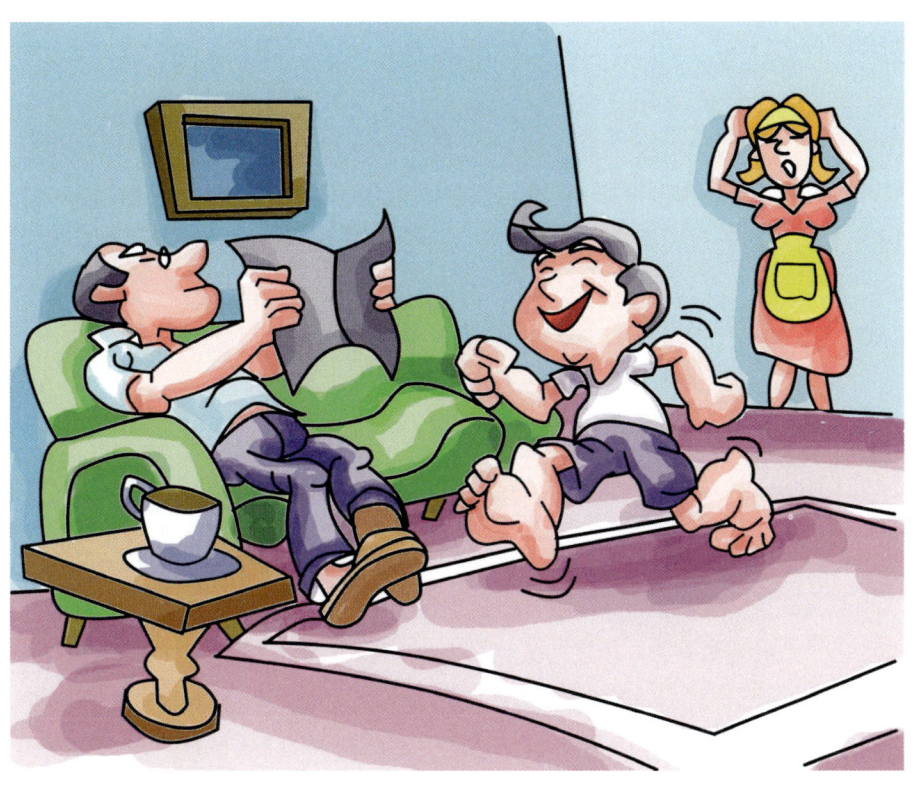

It's not alright to run with scissors.

Running with scissors is never a good idea. Nothing good can ever happen when you run with a pair of scissors. I know, because my brother ran with scissors and slipped and fell and snipped his earlobe in two and stuck the scissor in his little head. He's ok after lots of stitches. Scissors are for cutting paper and other things. Scissors are not meant for running. Just ask my brother.

It's not alright to spit.

Yech! That is what people think when you spit. Sidewalks are for walking or riding your skateboard or scooter. They are not for spitting. Did you ever step in someone's spit by mistake? Yuk! Or gum? Spitting is a nasty thing to do and you don't want to be nasty, do you? And don't we all love kisses? Mommy and Daddy don't like to give kisses to spitters. That's why it's not okay to spit.

It's not alright to talk to strangers.

There are lots and lots of people in the world. So many we can't even count them. Too many to even know who they are. Most of those people are good people like you. But a few are not good. So how do you know? Well, that's your grown-up's job. Your grown-up will decide who is safe to talk to. Your job is to not talk to someone you don't know. This can cause big, BIG trouble! You could get hurt or taken away from your family or WORSE! So don't talk to strangers, it's not okay.

It's not alright to throw rocks.

Sometimes, you think something inside your head that would be fun to do. Like pick up a rock and just throw it. When you think about it, it sounds fun! But it should stay inside your head. You should not throw rocks. All kinds of things could go wrong and then you would be in big, BIG trouble! Like breaking a window. Or conking somebody on their head. Or even hitting a bird as it flies by. No, nothing good can ever come from throwing rocks. That's why it's not ok.

It's not alright to throw things at people.

There are two kinds of throwing. Throwing 'to' and throwing 'at.' Throwing to is fun. It is for playing catch. Or tossing something to your friend. Throwing to is mostly okay. It is never a good thing to throw at someone. This can be dangerous and get you in big, BIG trouble! They could be hurt. You could hit them in the head or poke their eye out. Or they could get mad at you. We want people to like us and feel safe when we're around them. That is why it is not okay to throw things at people.

It's not alright to waste food.

Food is very important. It gives us energy to run and play. It helps us stay awake in class so we can get good grades. It helps us grow up big and strong. Every living thing needs food, even plants and bugs. Without food we would be tired and slow. We could not think well enough to get good grades. Eventually, if we did not eat we would die. And food costs money. More than your allowance. That's why it is not okay to waste food.

The End

Made in the USA
Middletown, DE
06 March 2020